DEEPEST THOUGHTS EXPLODING FROM AN EXPERIENCED WOMAN

BY AUTHORESS LADY R

Front cover by Chy Illustrations

Edited by I A.M. Editing, Ink

Book design by Authoress Lady R

Printed in the United States of America

ISBN: 978-1-7369465-1-0 (Paperback)

ISBN: 978-1-7369465-2-7 (Ebook)

CONTENTS

DEDICATION

To my kids, especially to my firstborn, my heart, and my right hand, my son Anthony (Pooh), this is for you. You gave me the strength to keep pushing and the best outlook on life and let me know it was okay to love. Continue to be the best in all you put your heart to and the big brother and role model to your siblings that I know you are. I love you, and this one is for you.

ACKNOWLEDGMENTS

First, giving honor to GOD, the head of my life. If it weren't for Him, I would not have kept the faith to go on.

To my mother, my right hand, the queen of my life, and the backbone, Peggy Smith, thank you for making me the woman I am today. Thank you for believing in me, giving me the push and encouraging words to go forth, and telling me I need to publish my work because of my talent.

Last but certainly not least, Felicia Williams, you believed in me when I didn't believe in myself. You believed that I had a story to tell with my skills of writing and stood by me proofreading even though you knew what it took to make me put pen to paper… lol

To the ones that led me to the right people, thank you. I love all of you in a special way.

FATHER

3 months of love
1 hour of sex
6 months later, a baby was in the mix
A mother left alone
A father now gone
Well, now mom, who went wrong?
You let him come and go as he pleased
While you're stuck at home raising me
He's sometimes there
Oh yes, a holiday
I never understand how things got this way
Sometimes I thought I was the reason
He couldn't stay
A full-time mom
A part-time dad
You know his existence in my life is truly sad
From a baby to a woman, you raised me
Where were you, dad?
Somewhere making another family!
FATHER

THE DAY HE DIDN'T CALL

The day he didn't call
I stayed in my room and stared at the wall
I loaned out my heart, and he refuses
Then all I ever get is more and more excuses
Sometimes I think I should have regretted the search
Should have left well enough alone and continued with my original
search
I've often felt my world was so very small
The day my father didn't call!

PATIENCE

Patience is time
It doesn't even cost a dime
There's no need to go around lying
Because it's too many people dying
Patience means to wait, not jumping from mate to mate
If that's the need, you should be locked up in a gate
Or lose out on something good, then it'll be too late
Patience is trust
If you don't, your love will rust
True love is not lust
You cannot sweep it away like dust
Love has got to have trust
Oh yes, this is real
It's a must
Patience is a virtue!!!!

Signed:

A Real Woman

ALONE

Long dark nights
Restless sleep
My eyes weep
Something's wrong
Why do I feel alone?
Nights, days, months by myself
The day my love left
My family pushed away
My love went far that day
Feelings now gone
And my heart now alone.

Signed:

A Real Woman

GET AWAY

I need peace of mind
I'm stressed out all the time
It's about that time to make that getaway
Dealing with the shit I'm dealing with every day
Got to find a place so I can hideaway
So I can be away from the madness
Far away from the noise and sadness
It's not too late
It's got to be a way to escape
All the nonsense
So much emotional pain
It's driving me insane
Part of the abuse
He treats me like my feelings don't ever matter
So what's the use?
I think love can be a pain
My head is going through a thang
Will I ever get treated with love and dignity?
Or will I be forever in reality?

Signed:

A Real Woman

WHY LIE?

Is it because you have nothing else better to do?
Or were you never taught to tell the truth?
You must not be scared of hell
'Cause that's where you're going to end up
By the lies you tell
So think before you say, "Heaven, goodbye."
Why Lie?
I must have never meant much to you
If so, you would never do as you do
I've learned to put myself first in my life
Instead of being stabbed in the back by a knife
So for now on, instead of hurting someone
Stop and take a deep sigh
THINK! WHY LIE?

Signed:

A Real Woman

WHY ME?

Why me?
I got to be the one always getting hurt
When you're the one always out trying to flirt
Why me?
I am the one who gives all my love to you
When we need to kneel down beside the church pew
Is it because I'm so kind?
Always have the right thing to say to leave you with a wandering
mind?
Why me?
Always trying to be there through thick and thin
No one to meet me halfway with a hand to lend
Is it because I ask for too much?
And instead of just being with me, you rather be with a bunch?
Why me?
The one that gets kicked in the ass
Then it runs out to be just a big joke and laugh
Can't you just tell me?
Instead of letting me see you don't love me?
You just love avoiding me
Why me?

Tired of being hurt, confused, and abused
And you don't know what you want; you're just confused
Always giving out love, never receiving it
And you just turn your back
And say go on b*t*h with that sh*t.
Just trying to be happily married
But no one there to share it
So I just keep thinking when
Who and Why Me?

WHAT'S LOVE?

Love is the way you feel
Love is the opposite of hate
Love does not envy
Love is honesty and obedient
Love is trust and respect
Love is what I feel
It never lies, never holds back
I give all of it as long as I'm met halfway
In order to receive love, you have to give love
Don't say those three words
Unless it's coming from the heart
Love can hurt
Love can kill
Love can be a night full of passion
Love can be a lifetime of pain
So MEAN IT
I Love You

Signed:

A True Black Woman

LOVE IS PAIN

Are you sure what you said is real?
Do you feel what you think you feel?
Are you sure your statements are true?
Should I fall back in love with you?
I want to in a way but then again
Should I?
I really want to stay
But then again, how could I?
I know now but didn't then
Got a different perspective now that we are friends
My whole state of mind thinks different
And everything was taken, not given
And now I know that what we had in love wasn't
And if it wasn't, I no longer trusted
'Cause love can hurt worse than pain do
It acts out of love and relationship brings pain too!

Signed:

Truth Hurts

CAN WE START OVER?

The fussing, fighting, and the raising hell
No longer is my heart for sale
Our love is just falling slowly, but shortly
Yet it'll be gone
And soon we'll both be so alone
You didn't think you was my number one lover
So can we just start all over?
My mind is racing with many thoughts
Of everything that has happened
I will not proclaim it is my fault
I admit when I have done wrong
You can do the same if you lift ya head and be strong
You used to be a dog, but ya name was not Rover
Give me ya hand and walk me so we can start over
Nobody truly wants to see us together
So we have to prove them wrong and make it last forever
This is not a fairy tale nor a dream
So take my ring and let's start our own team
There will be 3 of us with the power
Can you trust me?
Let's Start Over

Signed:

The One and Only

WHY I LOVE YOU

I love you because you care
Or is it that you're always there?
I love you because you have trusted in me
It's a feeling there I just can't seem to see
I love you because you're a strong but yet beautiful woman
My soul gets so hot, I need to be fanned
I love you because you're not shy
Therefore, I may even need a spy
I love your honesty
It's there, but I can't see it
Sometimes I don't feel that we're fit to be going through this shit
I love you through good and bad
But it seems like I'm the only one that ends up sad
Or with a child without a dad
I love you, and I know it's there
Instead of you being everywhere
You need to be here with me
So you can see the reason I love you
If not, I'll just let it be
And then I'll never know the answer to why I love you

Signed:

Renee Moffett

CRAZY IN LOVE

I ain't crazy in love
Just str8 (straight) insane
For the thought of your name
Bring thrills full of chills up and thru my veins
It brings tears to my voice
When I see the future of your face
And the straightness of your poise
Silence is golden when you step in the room
No one talks, walks, or dares to even move
It is the little things you do that help me realize
That life just ain't worth living if you ain't by my side
'Cause all these other girls can step and dismiss themselves
'Cause what you need is a real man
I'll complete your world
So stop your searching for rubies
It's a diamond right in your face
I may not be a 10, but trust me, I'm on the way!

Signed by:

A Real Black Woman

1 MORE X FOR OLD TIME SAKE

That love we had
The conversation was never bad
I remember that time
The different hotels we made love in
Fell asleep holding each other
I remember that time
When I paged or called or when I asked you to come by
I remember that time
The jokes we laughed at, the games we played
No arguing, no fussing, no problem
I remember that time
I worked, got off
Traveled distance to see you
No excuses and you met me there
We greet with a hug, a kiss
Not just walk pass
I remember that time
You said you'll love to move here
You'll love to be with me
No matter what happens
I remember that time

We told each other we cared
Enjoying the time we shared
Spent more time then than now
I remember that time
You holding me or holding you
Playing in your hair
No complaints
No acting like you didn't want to be touched
We wrestled, we played
I remember that time
No attitudes the time in the bathrooms the hotels
The floor the nights spent together no hurry here or there
Things were fun and worth remembering
Nowadays, I don't know
I would like that time once more, for old time's sake!
I don't have to take no more games and shit
You love me for me
That's the way it should be
You are so different from others
You are a one of a kind lover
Now I can lay my head and sleep in peace
Why?
I never knew a love like this!

Signed by:

A True Woman

MY TRUE FEELINGS

The tears are falling, but they're not going to bring you home
I can't take your hand to dry them up, and I can't move on
It's really not that easy
We started a family
But there's no one left to blame but me
I knew it was going to be trouble the minute you came at me
Why didn't I walk away from the start?
It's not my fault you that won't do your part
Leaving you is not something that I'm ready to do
I'm not going to win if I lose out on being with you
I'm not going to say good-bye
It's already hurt, so I know that it will be hard to try
Thinking of you being gone is killing me
Why can't you solve these problems willingly?
Take control of this situation for once in your life
I'm not asking for a ring; I'm not asking to be your wife
Just be true and honest with me for a change
Stop your lies
I'm about to have your child
There should be no shame
Be a father to our child instead of just a daddy

Spend time with your baby and not just spend dollars
All because you see another pretty face you think you should holla
Don't flush my true feelings down the drain
'Cause my true feelings for you will always remain the same!

Signed by:

A Real Woman

BABY DADDY DRAMA

Once I hit 5 months, you claimed I trapped you
Believe it or not, my idea of a good father is not you
But if only I knew then what I know now
This seed I'm carrying wouldn't be your child
Now I'm 9 months and the time sucks
So if I tried to trap you nigga, now you're fucked
Just my luck you don't give a fuck
But you gave a fuck when you gave that nut
I'm used to that baby daddy drama
I ain't trying to be your woman
Only your baby mama
So will it hurt you to give love to your flesh and blood?
Which is your child?
Matter of fact, your only one
You better show love to your only son

Signed:

Truth Hurts

ANTHONY

01-06-09 @ 10:03 PM

A = Anthony a fine young man, my son
N= Not second, but he's #1
T = The love from everyone he has won
H = He is not only my son; he's God's son
O = Once you think you're down, he'll bring you up
N == Not just Mr. Right; he'll hold you real tight
Y = You have to believe it; he's a light
With a smile from out of sight
I, his mom, will never leave him on any hot day or cold night

Signed:

A Real Woman

KHAMANI

K= Khamani, a handsome young man
H= He's my other son on this land
A= Away his mother took him and ran
M= My young man, I took and raised him to be
A= A smart and intelligent boy remembers everything he sees
N= Not just anybody's child
I= I pray since she took him, he doesn't grow to be wild!

Signed by:

Renee

I CAN'T EXPLAIN!

I can't explain the way you make me feel
I wish our relationship was real
But you're steady playing games and leading me on
You not going to feel the pain until I'm gone
I stayed by your side, good times and bad
Now it seems you want to throw away what we had
Of course, I love you
I'm not so sure you love me
I hate how complicated this relationship is about to be
It's like I'm sprung over you, but you don't care nothing about me
How much time do we have to wait
Before you actually see
That life ain't easy, especially for me?
Because I'm without you
And that's the part that's killing me
You don't understand how I cry
Thinking of all the heartbreak and lies
I tried. God knows I tried
But you looking at it from only one side
Frankly, I'm tired of wasting my time
Either you're staying with me, or you're not

When I'm asking you questions, you steady saying I forgot
This bullshit is fucking my brain
And how I feel for you, I just can't explain

SIGNED BY:

A MAD BLACK WOMAN

WHY & WHEN

Why is it every time someone ask for a little cash
You turn right around and ask for some ass?
When was the last time
You actually gave me a dime?
When was it you did anything without me asking?
This proves why our love wasn't everlasting
Do you honestly believe it's better to give than receive?
No, that's probably why you're always being deceived
Do you know for real what you really want in life?
Is it to be a hoe or a real woman to be ya wife?
Well, this is not a game 'cause my heart is really in pain
So either you give respect, or someone is going to be very hurt and
disrespected
Believe it or not, it's easy to do right then wrong
'Cause it's not easy being single and grown
Why is it hard to forget about the past
And stop putting me last?

Signed by:

Renee Moffett

WHY LOVE HURTS

Love hurts in so many ways
Love can last for minutes, hours, or days
It can make your heart clutter
When it ends, it can feel you're in a shutter
It's a shame to been hurt so many times
You can count it to a hundred by dimes
And then you don't know if you'll find the special one
You don't want to ever think of turning back the hands of time
Love hurts so badly
You'll think you wrote the song "You Got It Bad."
When love hurts, you may feel like shit
Then the next person says they love you
You'll think, what has love got to do with it
It's just a bitch
Love can hurt where every night you go to bed and cry
Then when the sun rises, you ask over and over why
It's just a shame
You point to every man and blame
You don't want to live on wondering why
So you sometimes just want to die
And just tell all the pain goodbye

You would like to know why all men lie
Because they think they can get away with it
So just act shy
Don't worry about love hurting you
It doesn't feel nice
So be single and forget the shit
Love Hurts Bad!!!

Signed by:

A Real Woman

WHY DID IT HAPPEN TO ME?

Why did it have to happen to me?
Is it because I was too blind to see?
Why can't this pain die?
Or am I just living a lie?
I rather be
"Men At Large, So ALONE,"
Instead of just feeling alone
Open my eyes and see
Why did it have to happen to me?
Happiness is not what I'm about to be
It's just I or My instead of all Us or We
I'm always out bending back
When all and all I should put it on a rack
This is not me, or did I let it be
What it turned out to be?
This lifestyle is not supposed to be my life
It should be deadened by a knife
Now I can open my eyes to see
Why did it happen to me?

WHY DID IT HAVE TO HAPPEN TODAY?

Why did it have to happen today?
I didn't want it to end this way
After realizing we have given it our last try
We finally said our last goodbyes
As a tear fell from my face
I started to cry for
Something we worked on for so long
It's just like the wind is gone
I didn't know life could be so unfair
This pain and sorrow I never thought I would have to bear
So as we give the final kiss goodbye
You wipe the tears from my eyes
We had so much planned for the future
But the past wouldn't let it last
As you walk away, I turn to say
Even though we're apart
You'll always have a special place in my heart
Why? Tell me why it had to happen today?
I didn't want it to end this way

IF I KNEW

If I knew it would be the last time
I'd see you fall asleep
I would tuck you in more tightly and pray your soul to keep
If I knew it would be the last time
I'd see you walk out the door
I'd give you a hug and kiss and call you back for just one more
If I knew it would be the last time
I'd hear your voice lifted up and pray
I'd videotape each action and word
So I could play them back day after day
If I knew it would be the last time
I would spare an extra minute to stop and say
I love you
Instead of assuming you know I do
If I knew it would be the last time
I would be there to share your day
I'm sure you'd have so many more
So I could just let this one slip away
For surely there's always tomorrow to make up for an oversight
We always get a second chance
To make everything just right

It will always be another day to say
I love you
Finally there's another chance
To say is there anything I can do
But just in case I might be wrong
And today is all I get
I'd like to say how much I love you
And make sure you never forget
Tomorrow is not promised to anyone young, old, light, or dark
And maybe today is the last day to hold your loved one tight
So if you're waiting for tomorrow, why not do it today?
For tomorrow never come surely we rest a day
You did not take that extra time for a smile
Hug or kiss
And you was too busy to grant someone
What turned out to be their one last wish
So hold your loved one close today and whisper in their ear
Tell them how much you love them, and you'll always hold them dear
If you take the time to say I'm sorry
Please forgive me
Thank you
I love you
Or it's ok
So if tomorrow never comes, you'll have no regrets about today

IF TABLES WERE TURNED

If the tables were turned
I would be the one out drinking all night
Then I wouldn't be right
If the tables were turned
I would be the one always with the head up high
Instead of the one letting out a sigh
If the tables were turned
I would be the one always needing or wanting and counting
Leaving you without shit
If the tables were turned
I wouldn't be the one losing and feeling depressed and all alone
I would be the one working and always gone
If the tables were turned
I would be the one that has no love
For the person that loved me and then
I would open up my eyes to see that it's a shame
To know how it would feel if the tables were turned
And that you don't miss a good thing until it's gone

GOT TO MAKE A CHANGE

It comes a time in everyone's life
They may even want to take their life by using a knife
Some may even want to think about killing their husband or wife
Not even thinking once that they may have to do jail time, perhaps life
It sometimes feels you're in a cage
When you should be influencing peers on somebody's stage
But instead, you have family and friends in court on the front pew
And eyes are on you
Not knowing now thinking about that reason your life is going to
And why you didn't stop to listen to those words you were told
Only that last breath you can't hold 'cause your days are now cold
GOT TO MAKE THAT CHANGE

NO MORE

I used to be in love with you
But not no more
You used to mean the world to me
Shit, not no more
I once put you first
I won't make that mistake no more
I gave you my all in everything
Not no more
Everyone said we were meant to be
They won't tell that lie no more
We shared everything together
We had hell
Won't do that no more
Jeffrey Osborne said, "Love's Gonna Last."
That was old people
Not no more
We used to make love all day and night
Can't do that no more
Used to plan the future
Ain't gotta worry about that no more
I used to keep you on my mind all the time

Forget that
Not no more
I wanted to have ya child
Damn, not no more
You made it do what it do like Jamie Foxx
You can't handle this no more
Took you back over and over again
I BETCHA LIKE HELL I WON'T DO THAT NO MORE!

Signed by:

A Real Woman

END OF THE ROAD

Stop your playing
Bullshit is what you're saying
You messed up and got set up
Now you locked up in your jail cell thinking, what the hell
Damn, does all love fail?
Oh well
Now it's 30 years
That's what your case is facing
Your mind is now spacing
Over the calendar days you'll be tracing
What about your kids?
And your little baby?
I see they'll be fatherless
Maybe it's cool
I'm not going to act shady
I see you don't care
Now your life ain't gone nowhere
Are you at the end of the road
Well, you could say I told you so!

Signed by:

Renee

THE END

It started off fine and dandy
It was walks on high land
Beautiful as flowers and a box of candy
Now it's worse than a one night stand
Hurt one heart to learn in reality
Mine was put out to get hung and bruised
Dreams told so well too
I'm yet still waiting for that love cruise
Instead, it's still a hit in the face that left a bruise
How much more can one heart bear?
Mine has had its last wear and tear
There's not any more love to share
My eyes can't water, so instead it's a glare
Let's just kiss and say goodbye
My hand for help I can bend
Don't look me in my eye
'Cause now this is the final end

Signed

An Angry Woman

THE VERY NEXT TIME!

My heart won't get hurt
By no one that is a flirt
I can sit and enjoy a bottle of wine
The very next time
High in the air will be my nose
Red polish on my toes
Something I won't have time for is
Holds up on my face
A smile will shine on the very next time
No fighting, cursing, or abuse
My kindness won't be misused
It will be perfect the next time
Wine and fine dining next time
Not this time
No, 'cause it won't be
A very next time
Next time!!!!

Signed By:

An Angry Woman

FREE AT LAST

No more heartaches
No more pain
Not at all stressed
Alone but I'm not ashamed
No more fear nor answering to no one
The phone calls, lies, and begging to leave me alone
No more dwelling on the past
'Cause now I am free at last
Love is a fool
I'm not gonna be put on the back burner or a pedal stool
No more worrying if everything is gonna be cool
No more bruises, scars, or even a body cast
Now I can keep my head up and stay on task
It feels good to be free at last!
Free at last... That I am!!!!

MY WIFE TO BE

Love at first sight
I knew she might be Ms. Right
We argue, laugh, and even have a little fight
One day I got to take time and see
If she's perfect for me
Is she my wife-to-be?
Her smile, her looks, and her style
I got to bring her over to my lifestyle
If I give her a lot, she'll stay for a while
Neither her nor me, it will become we
Her heart I must soon hold the key
Then I know she'll be my wife to be
She who holds my heart in her hand
Thank God she's not a man
'Cause he would never make it
Past being just a friend
Soon will take our family and leave
A promise was made and said just wait and see
Will soon be each other's wife
Instead of just a wife-to-be!!!!

Signed:

A Real Woman

MY HEART

I feel so full of love
My first birds are two turtledoves
It's beating so fast and strong
Where am I going wrong?
I want to keep you close and love you for a lifetime so long
My heart!!!!
Let's travel to the seven seas
Let me love you like the birds and the bees
If this not what you want
Let me know
I promise I won't cry and put on a show
For the last time, lay down and let me go low
My heart
Everything, put it in my hands
Let me take away the worry
This loves gonna last, so no need to hurry
My kids, my wife, my love is all I care about
Meet me halfway
It's only fair
Don't make me wait long 'cause my heart

The pain it cannot bear
My heart

Signed:

A Real Woman

A NEW LIFE

A new home, a new state, and a new start
I packed up my life, my family, and from Chicago we depart
I had to leave the past behind and go somewhere fresh to unwind
Ever since my aunt was laid to rest
I felt like I was living in such a mess
So to fix the hole in my heart
That was made by the love knife
I left to start over fresh a new life
A change is going to come
Soon we'll have another little one
We will start over and things that we build
We can call our own
When we're done, we'll take it, and to the haters, it will be shown
That we may better for ourselves and stay together
Just me, my son, and my wife
Together we shook the haters and proved them wrong
And started a brand new lifeline

Signed:

A Real Woman

NEVER KNEW

Never knew a love like this
That can snatch me up by the wrist
One that can sweep me off my feet
Can make my heart speed up a beat
Never knew a love like this
My love is not at risk
My soul soon will be taken
It seems like my heart was never broken
Never knew a love like this
I can put you number one on my list
When you kiss me, it makes my lips quiver
When you touch me
You make my entire body shiver
Never knew a love like this

A BEAUTIFUL WOMAN

A smile that will make you blush
When she calls, you may want to rush
So pretty and bright
If you could love her, you just might
A beautiful woman
The perfect personality
Will make you ask if this reality
Maybe in your eyes she's a waste of time
But this woman right here is more than a dime
She will blow your damn mind
A beautiful woman
A body shaped like a Coca Cola bottle
She will make you holla
A friend my friend and understandable friend
So to all men
You might want to know who I'm talking about now
I'm about to let you know
When she's done doing her show
You can now get on one knee
And say can you please marry me
A beautiful woman named Ebonii

THIS WOMAN'S BLACK PRIDE

The lady that has strong black pride
Has the greatest joy in stride
Without this woman, some souls could have died
This loved one told us to shut up and come along for the ride
She's the pride in my life
Also Veronica spans one an only wife
This lady plays a very important part
And three beautiful kids lives
She brings a smile to many, especially to me and my wife
So please don't mistake her for any shyness
Nor take her kindness for weakness
She runs around doing so much for others
Still young but has more parenting skills than those who claim to be
mothers
She has a heart that's worth more than gold
A lie she may have told
With her voluptuous full-figured body, she stands bold
So much trust
My heart, my life
And my kids are placed in her hands to hold

To all that know who I'm bragging about
Let's stand up and shout
Don't cry; dry your eyes
I love you Nikki Scarver

MY SISTER

A smile that will make you blush
An attitude that will give you rush
Her eyes so pretty and light
If you love her, you just might
When you need her, she's there
No matter if you're lost anywhere
Maybe in your eyes she's a waste of time
But this one right here is more than a dime
Huh, she blew Dre's mind
That's why she's a sister of mine
I may not have known her very long
But she's never misled me wrong
She has a heart that's bigger than the world
You know if you're older than a carefree curl
A woman, a strong black woman
A free your mind woman
And there is no one better than her
The first thing you'll buy her
Is a thousand dollar fur
Independent she is because she got her own
If you need it, doesn't mind giving a loan

I love her as if she was truly a part of me
This woman, my sister
My heart in a loved one
Her name is Katie
My sister

WHAT'S A TRUE FRIEND?

A person that's always there
Someone who really cares
Runs to you on wet or dry land
Is there really a true friend?
No matter how far or near
They always lend an ear
'Til you don't ask when
You know you can
What is a true friend?
Never turned their back on you
Every word that comes out may sound so true
Picks you up out of the sand
Now is this a true friend
Will give you their last or first
Fixed the well when you thirst
The one who gives you a shirt off their back
Picks up in the places you may slack
Their name may not be Kim, Toya, Aaron, or even Sharon
But my definition of a true friend
Her name is the one and only Kerrin...

LOVERS & FRIENDS

You can't be serious to put a smile upon my face
When you place your small hands on my full-figured waste
The way the tip of your tongue made me feel good all over
No way will we remain just friends
My heart yearns to be your number one lover
When you're mad, sick, or even hurt
If your body is bare
Off my back, I will give you my baby fat shirt
That cold fair night in January felt like
We were the only ones that walked the land
Made me feel like Deborah Cox and RL
If we couldn't be lovers, we sure the hell were no longer be friends
The words I love you form so serious in your mouth
Just me, you, and our kids living
Beautiful in the far South
A new addition I give to you
Upon my finger, you place a ring to cover
A life just beginning with a destined-to-be lover
No one ever made me feel the way you do
Just by the sound of your voice
My body for you to do as you please

To satisfy the pleasure of your choice
The love we share is not only unbreakable
But side-by-side untouchable we stand
Two people, two hearts
We share the unforgettable meaning of lovers
But yet true friends...

THE STORY SHE TOLD

She's beautiful inside and out
She's been lied on, cheated on, even talked about
A wonderful, talented dancing performer
Smile so bright, skin so pure
Make up was never a necessity to transform
Heart shines right and is as big as gold
Far as I'm concerned, no lies she has never told
My mommy always told me to be like Milira
A one-man woman
She told the last story
Like Shirley Brown did to Barbara Mason in "Woman to Woman."
Sick and all, she went to work and did her job as the HBIC of the mic
Strong and proud
Never kept too many in her circle
'Cause more than three is a crowd
When she got tired of being pushed, shoved, and pulled
That's when she cut her hair and gave Fantasia a try
And said it's all good
When I was down and out, she would tell me to let go and let God
I'd just to hear her say fix it, Jesus
Ohmygod

Wommack and Wommack said, "Baby, I don't understand it."
Indigo Blue said, "Try Jesus. He'll tell you all about it."
The million-dollar question was, "Jangalang jangalang. Which way
does it hang?
"Indigo Blue jiggalicious 70s diva," says mom
Sisters, brothers, and my extended family
Please, no more crying
God has me now
And I have no more pain
Her last words to me were, "Mommy loves you."
But God shined on us all and said
"She must go on without you."

BONNIE AND CLYDE

I was the Bonnie to your Clyde
No stories, never lied
I stand by your side
With beauty and pride
Never lovers and friends
You left me allowed to stand
On a hard but gloomy land
By myself with no caring hand
Tears fell upon my pillow
Not once have I seen your shadow
You were always under my halo
I wore red; you wore yellow
Unbreakable we were
Distance far as the sun from the glistening star
So much hate in pain
I cry so many tears
There's no need to go outside in the rain

A HEART THAT'S COLD

The lies, being used
It all gets tiresome and old
One can ruin it for all
And turn a once beautiful heart into a heart that's cold
All the faking, the teasing
Believing the love is pure as gold
Remember it was your lust and games
That caused this story to be told
I gave put my heart, mind, body, and soul in your hand to hold
In return, slowly but surely, the fakeness began to unfold
I was blinded by love
Failed to see the signs that showed
When you cry, I cry
When you hurt, I'm hurt
Someone pissed you off
I was on cloud 9
Pacing the floor, ready to hit the road
The walls made of steel around a heart that's now cold
In need of a way to let off this heavy load
Being a whore is not a sign of being bold
Having your cake and eating it too is fun

That's actually the best damn lie told
Playing with a person's heart will get you murked
And when it's all said and done
You'll be laying in a puddle of your own pureblood
Annual be an example of what happens
When a beautiful heart of gold has now turned to a heart that's
so cold

CHANGE

This pain I'm feeling from your heart
The way you try to flirt
Tears all over my white shirt
Move around apologies no longer work
I travel to you sunshine or rain
The stab in my back left a bloody red stain
Your love had me higher than a crack head off pure white cocaine
The hurt you had has no fiery against this pain
If I no longer see you, I would put up no fuss
Your love toward me has turned out to be lust
The constant ringing has finally become a hush
When slippery, I will pay to have you hit by a CTA bus
I wish you were the target at the gun range
So once you're out my life how easy it would be to make this change
Sometimes it takes the worst pain
To bring about the best change

UNTIL THERE WAS YOU

While I lay here waiting to hear from you
I can't help thinking about what my life has become
When you became a part of it
Waiting and wanting you have been the focus of my thoughts
these days
Knowing that one day all that I have envisioned of us being together
will finally happen
Even if it's just for a moment
You give me a reason to wake up in the morning and smile
Just smile for no particular reason
Except for the fact that you aren't here
As days go by, I feel myself growing closer and closer
My heart is suddenly coming out of its shy spot
Wanting to feel what it feels like to be loved again
I don't ever want to lose this feeling
I don't ever want to lose you
When I hear your voice
It's like a feeling I don't want to leave
You give me comfort and joy
The sound of your voice is like my favorite love song
I can listen to it all night until it puts me to sleep

Yet, as I continue to lay here and think about everything you are
to me
Still, I just want you to know that wherever this road may take us
And how far it may be to finally get where we want to go
Always know you are in my heart, and in my heart is where you will
always be
Life hasn't been this grateful to me
Until there was you
Thank you for being you
What I'd like to say next
I'd like to say to you personally until then

THE PERFECT WOMAN

A lady that always keeps her nails and hair done
She always knows that she's number one
She has her own job
Own house and her own car
The woman you'll never find in nobody's bar
She walks with her head far in the sky
'Cause she knows she's all that
She walks past
You have to take three steps back
The perfect woman
A woman that will make you love her
When you see her, the first thing you do is lay down your
hundred-dollar fur
The lovemaking she always have will make you give her mom a
high five
This woman is not any woman
She will make you laugh like a hyena
Independent, yes that she is
But this is the perfect woman
Diana

WE

I searched until I found these roses in my color blue
So magical and eye-pleasing, especially for you
The uniqueness of these roses are truly one of a kind
And the uniqueness of this Queen is simulating to your mind
So is it you that deserve these roses
And this beautiful glass vase?
Of course, you do, my Queen
I only wish to see your face
I know your lips are smiling
Is it me that made you blush?
I can see appreciation beating your heart
No need for words, so baby hush
These roses are to be given only on special occasions
So you are Mz. Special
In my book, my sexy motivation
There's a love story on my soul, and yes, you are the star
You belong up in the sky next to heaven
And no matter how far the distance we have become
It's because I'm working on me
Trying to get my life in order

So I can change that me to
WE

THIS FEELING I FEEL

This feeling I feel is not right
My love for you is further than sight
You made love to me
My smile was brighter than the sunlight
A sudden change happened in just one single night

This feeling I feel is so strong
I know loving you is wrong
Our love is destined to last long
We will be side by side nail to the throne

This feeling I feel is so bold
My heart was old
Forever is what you showed

This feeling of love is bound by Christ
Will have the biggest wedding no matter the price
I promise to be by your side as your one and only wife

If it takes the rest of my life to make sure I got it right
I'll make sure that forever is real
Just promise me I'll never lose this feeling that I feel

MOUNTAIN PEAK

For me, this year has been a special mountain
Incandescent when it suddenly peaks
Revisiting its rich eventful days
So full of love is one more gift from you
New love, there is no darkness on our lovely mountain
As I gaze upon my life from this peak
Nothing I imagined matches
Needing, wanting, loving, and having you
In earlier years, I thought of this first mountain
Visioning the Vista from its peak
Each thought was there
Even in those days
Ripples in the darkness without you
So shall I love you on this yearly mountain
As I cast a quick glance backward from its peak
Recalling the long innocence of days
Yearning for what I now have in you

A LOVE 2 HEARTS SHARE

The joy of starting off as friends
After walking the same pride land
With just knowing of each other's BOSS name

A type of love two ears share
A bond so tight
The unthinkable wouldn't even dare

Whether near or far together or apart
Cold or in heat
The closest enemy would get their ass beat

Time we share feels so right
Both smiles shine so bright
Without you, there is no me

When the time is right
Truly the world will soon see

The best relationship is starting as friends first
So many years arguing and cursing
The meant to be true love of yours
I always thirst to be

The late-night dinner dates
Long walks by the breezy lake
Your soft lips on me every morning when I wake
The ring I placed upon your finger you proudly take

Vow before God my wife
The Bishop will make

BE MY LADY

Whenever I think about you
I can't resist
So baby, let me give you all
My love and tenderness

Girl, every time I see you, I wish I tried
Maybe you would have said yeah
And been here by my side

When you smile at me
You look like an angel
Sent from above
Baby, all I want to do
Is give you all my love

I will show you my love
In different ways
But the problem is
When I try to tell you, I just don't know what to say

If you are my girl, I would be there whenever you call
So now I will end this one and for all
Baby, will you be my lady?

FOR MY HUSBAND

You are the first sight in the morning
My last sight at night
For you, my heart has always been longing
You've changed my world so much
From the first special kiss and your soft, gentle touch
Forever I will smile like this

We met over ten years ago
8 brilliant first two years it has been

My, where does the time go?
It was such a big space between
We fought through it
Although I always seemed mean
It was all worth it
When I'm able to get a hug from you
It makes me so happy, and I feel wanted

I love all that you do

Some I may take for granted
But nothing can be stronger
Than my love for you
The love we have is blissful
Even though we have our ups and downs
No one can come between this

Our smiles and our frowns
When we kiss and cuddle
All the frowns from hurt seemed to drown.

THE FIRST LOVE OF MY LIFE

Without your love, my dear, I would not be here
For I wouldn't be the person I am today
You supported me, and you loved me unconditionally
I felt so unworthy
Scorned because of my past
On me, you don't and have never turned your back
That's what makes me stronger
Knowing your love for me gives me the strength to fill it
See it after being tested so many times
I'm glad you are all mine
The persistence you show me gives me my final answer
You will love me
Like nobody else can
Everlasting love
That is what I prayed to the Lord above
You are my saving grace
Without you by my side, I would feel out of place
Not in this place if this is where I am supposed to be
The place where I belong
On the right of you forever

And really that's not very long
I will love you with all my heart
I'm glad you found a place for me in your heart!

TAKE AWAY THE PAIN

I'm hurting so deep inside
I put all the past behind
'Cause if I didn't, my heart would have exploded nationwide
Never would I like to rewind it
Felt like I was going insane
I'm glad to know he can take away the pain
Now here it is what I've always been told
My mother stood up bright and bold
Child, pick it up and read
Don't just follow; take the lead
Just ask, and you shall receive
I didn't talk back; I just took heed
I had plenty of faith
Needed somebody to tell
I could not wait
I asked my God from my heart with no shame
Please take away the pain
He answered, "Put it in my hand and let it go
Get on your knees and pray loud, not real low.
Lay and go to sleep with no worries."

And your mind is saying
"When morning comes, I won't tell you
But you will feel that I did what you asked, child.
I've taken away every single pain."
God's child

HE'S COMING BACK

When?
We will never know
Every day something happens to show
He makes the wind blows
Every day someone gets sick
And go
We never know what the weather may be the next day
All we know is he's coming back, He says
So every night, I lay and pray
Every moment I get up, I put my lips to pray
So you may tell many lies
As he subtracts the days you may rise
You're fine some going against one of the 10 commandments
Wearing rings yet out doing unworthy things
To steal, connive, and kill
Are not part of God's will
So I'm saying get your life steady
And yet be ready
Because I'm letting you know now
Because I got to go

His name is Jesus, not Jack
He's coming back

Signed by:

Renee

TEARS OF A BROKEN HEART

These tears are falling fast
I thought our love would last
We cannot go on living in the past
My heart is so broken underneath this cast

Too many years off and on
Love that was once there is now gone
Your anger and hate you have shown
Heartache and pain is enough
No need for a broken bone

Mental and physical abuse
On my heart, I wear
How much do you think one heart can bear?
Day in and day out, you live without one single care
Everybody can see that we're no longer a pair

I will never forget, but I will always forgive
Miserable and stressed
I no longer can live
I'm never sleep before the clocks strike 12
Need you to believe that tears of a broken heart is real

Signed:

A Real Woman

ADDICTED

Your lips, your touch, I can't deny
When you're gone, I miss you
That's no lie
What did you do to me?
I constantly ask why
That day you approached me
No need to act shy

While my knees were yet bended
Yes, my pearl stuck out from behind
You licked it
In the backseat with the windows tinted
Your sex appeal
I admit I'm addicted

Every minute every hour
Is filled with love and fun

Leave if you please
Forever you'll dream about the pearl tongue
You cheat the hole in your chest
I placed from my hot .45
Let's make this family extended
On my hand, you placed a diamond pendant
I will love you for eternity
Because to your love, I'm so addicted

LORD

Though we strive to be together, we're apart
Reasons being we don't know
The feelings we do show seems like forever
But it's only been almost a year
And trust ironically is our only fear
Why we do not trust
I do not know
I care about her in the strongest way
And if she asked me to marry her
I would say OK
I am hers, and she is mine
She will always be my baby
I know she has two, but she cares for both
There is not just one
She cares for the most
Lord, what should I do in this tangled tree
If she is undecided on whether or not she wants to be with me?

Signed by:

Love Hurts

LOVE ALL OVER ME

It's bigger than the world
Drops wetter than a carefree curl
Everyone ought to try it
If not, please believe it
I don't want to cover it
'Cause it's love all over

Holds me close night and day
No one can ever get in the way
I don't never have to pay
But I always do pray
It's a one of a kind lover
You may want to try this love all over

He has my lovely brother
This love is like no other

You really want to know who I'm bragging about
'Cause I have no fear to speak pf him out loud
Open your eyes and see this glow He gave me
My Jesus has love all over me

EVERY WIFE'S DESIRE

Let me be motivation
Inspiration in the air between
Let me be the reason you smile
The one who changes your frown upside down
Let me be the one who you look up to and admire
Your soul desire
Let me be the rumble in your heart, not the hole in your ear
Telling you everything you need, not just wanting to hear
Let me be the one who means so much
To you be your answer to life's ups and downs
Let me make you need me every single morning when you're awake
Especially when you, my dear, have had enough
Let me make your excitement
When you kiss me goodnight
After the day was rough
Let me want all these things from you
While knowing you are the one who gets me through
Let me love you more
In each and every way, it's true
I'll let you bless me with life made by us

Give all things from you
Knowing my every treasured desire as your wife

SECOND TO NO ONE

I'm the only girl
Getting your heart
But your body's an issue
I must depart
I'm your only lady
I don't understand your logic
I come first
Don't want to be another topic
When you come in at night
You lay down next to me
And when we make love
Who makes you moan so easily?
You have got to understand to never leave
I will take you as is
Though you cheated on me
You mean that much to me
Even more than gold, I know you feel the same
Because I'm the only girl you hold
You kiss me in places you never thought you would
You would never hurt me even though you could

My whole body tingles when you call my name in that special kind
of way
And my whole body jerks when we're under covers every day
On top of tables
On top of chairs
On the counter
On our way up the stairs
On the bed
Against the headrest
And you just said I was your best
In your car
Cruise control
Sex so good
Both our bodies roll
Hot and wet
Steamy sex
Lips on neck
Now we're set
You need me
And I need you
When we are under
It's just us two
No distractions
Unlimited love
No restrictions
UN me
For the world to see
In my heart in my soul
Best fantasy won
Always number one
Never ever second to none

LIFE'S A STRUGGLE GAME

Shake the dice
Join the game
Life for you
Will never be the same

Why turn and look back?
Lost all respect in time
What you have
The largest mountains to climb

Bullet in your head
Red blood you shed
Trembling in the hospital bed
By the game you led

Your body suddenly stops
Rest of the world flowing
No mind to think
Time still going

Back to dice
The game God will roll
Wake up; start a new life
Finished with mind, body, and soul

THE STRONG MOTHER I KNOW

Never got her first case
Women she idolized
Never felt love's bliss
Sexy body all over
Yet paralyzed

Never taught to dance
Or go to the prom
Never got the chance
Won't ever forget where she came from

Wasn't able to say to her first love, "I do."
Ship far, far away
Strong mother, I know

Arms couldn't reach to comb her hair
Not able to grasp her hands
She couldn't squeeze you, dear
Wasn't able to understand
Couldn't put makeup on her beautiful face
No strength for a loving embrace

Tears in the middle of prayer
Assistance given by a wheelchair
No show of any fears
Shadow ears to any cries
Dehydrated to form moist tears
Only redness covered her eyes

Speechless to talk
No sympathy from you
Gave up on the walk
Never look for pity
That's why she'll always be
The strongest black mother I've ever known

COLD COLD HEART

The world so cold
My heart now shattered
All the young ones never old
Young girls abused and battered

Young, innocent hearts taken
Treated wrong and mean
Families' hearts bruised and shaken
Every morning they wake, wishing it was all a dream

The blood on my shirt
The day you were taken
Little Nicole went missing
Started the Amber Alert
Her mother's tears forsaken
Broad daylight babies
Lives were taken so bold

So many bullets with tips of gold
Day by day, the number gets larger
That's why sending our kids to school gets harder

This world is getting colder
After so many years, we got a black president
Once and for all, did we really get change?
It really doesn't matter where you choose your residence
Every morning you wake
Channel 7, 9, and 11 bring a different kind of pain

No one knows what is going on
Did it really start at home?
Old sayings went like
Can we all get along?
That was slavery days
When you felt that way
Now cops killing you
Just for traffic stops
Or the fact that you didn't change your tone

It doesn't matter if you didn't say your grace
'Cause it's not the opposite race
It's our own kind killing each other
Pray before you step out tomorrow in this cold world
'Cause black lives don't matter

If it did, instead of taking another life,
You'd try loving one another

HEAVEN GATES

Lord help me believe
For whatever may I be
And all that I am
Show me heavens' stairway
I hear bells ringing all day
I have to climb
Lord, for my sake
I will fear no evil
Teach me how to take one day at a time
The sky breaks
It breathes upon my face
In the presence of my enemies
The world below is full of enemies
Lord, when I wake
The clouds of heaven gate
There is no, not one safe place I rather be

BEAUTIFUL WHITE ROSE

A red rose whispers of passion
The white rose breathes of love
For the red one is a Falcon
Beautiful white roses is a dove

I send you a pearl white rosebud
Flushed on its petal tips
For the love that is purest and loving
Has a kiss of desire on my lips

CONTENTMENT IN REALITY

May I find little contentment?
On the tip of the mountain crest
Or beside the wide blue lake
That rested on its breast

In a quiet elves Glen
Besides the drizzling reels
Contemplating giant green trees
Above God's eternal hills

Maybe where sunlight
Falls an iridescent glow
Between the leaves of Bella's trees
On top the grass below

It's not beside the lake
Neither top of mountain peaks
Or the valley far below
The increase that I seek

After the search has ended for sure
I will find contentment in reality
Probably just a bad state of mind

DEAR MOTHER

Everything I am is because of you
You are the first voice that ever sang to me
At every turn, you push me to go further
You teach me to be true to myself and the ones that I love
When I look into your eyes, I am so proud
Because of you, I am the woman I am today
Now that I am a mother
I truly realize all the sacrifices you made for us
My love for you is far beyond all that I can say
I love you in such a special way
A bond of mother and daughter nobody can take away

YOU CALLED MY NAME

Baby momma
I am sorry
So sorry
I know now
You called out my name
The night you left me
Plies started barking

It was so late
I was half asleep
I figured nothing was wrong, so why bother
Something outside stirred up Plies
We know how he is
The slightest breeze and he's yapping

I laid there
I thought it was my imagination

That you called out to me
Soon after, Plies quickly settled down
So I fell back to sleep
I should have answered you
Checked up on you
Then maybe I would have witnessed your departure instead
I found you dead 3 hours later

A BLESSING TO YOUR SOUL

You may recognize within your life
The presence of power and light in our soul

You may realize that you are never alone
That your soul's brightness and belonging
Connects intimately to the rhythm of the universe

May you have all respect for your own individuality and soul

May you even realize that the shape of your soul is unique
That you have a special destiny here
That behind the façade of your life
There is something beautiful, good, an eternal happening

May you learn to see yourself with delight, pride, and expectations
With which God sees in every soul

FANTASY DREAM

Watch waves beat the sand
On the rock, we were hand in hand,
The waves crash down
As I wiped away my frown

When the sun starts to set
Feels like we've just met
We've known each other for quite a while
It used to be just the thought of you makes me smile

We began to walk
Then started to talk
The night steps in sync
So many thoughts can't even think

This man stops and looks at me
When I look up, he is all I see
He leans in, but it's like the perfect sense

As I always wake up and realize
It was just a fantasy dream

DEMONS OVERMIND

I don't believe that anyone kills themselves by suicide
You get to a point in your life
Where it hurts to breathe
Point where you can't stand thinking of waking up in the morning
It's not you inside your head anymore

Demons have taken over your conscience
Every piece of our mind that's left
He controls every single thought
All your actions and every single word you say

Finally, this point in time
Maybe you have lost yourself completely
Now willing to do just about anything and anything at all
To banish the demons out of your mind

Demons all by themselves bring blades
To your wrist every single time
They make you open bottles of pills
Make you swallow not one or a couple
But every last one

Demons load the 35-millimeter gun
Cock it back as well
They tie the rope to make a noose
Make your feet jump off the stool

Once they're finished with you
Not a single sign of breath
Then you'll find your soul more alive than ever before
Just maybe then you will find peace within you

I DON'T, I JUST

I don't know how to let you in without feeling judged
I just don't know how to tell you how broken I am
Without the needy feeling

How do I cry without my tears feeling like acid?
I want you to see that I'm hurting
Without me telling you

All my words are bleeding out of my mouth
Waiting for you to stitch it up and make me fine
Although I know that's no longer your job
Even though you're better off away and without me
I'm drowning in this wine
I just need you to see me one last time

FINALLY I'VE BLOWN

Soul
Falling from the gray sky
I'm never afraid to die
Why?
I've finally flown

This wind sounds so much like your voice
The last time we talked
I couldn't grow wings
But your voice convinced me to jump

When I met you
I told my inner self never to fall in love
But my soul, as usual, doesn't obey my mind
So where are we left tonight?
Why?

I have finally flown
Why don't you come find me
Where the sun and the sky don't know each other?

I'll meet you along the edge
And we'll fly together

FALLING NOISE

Throughout the world
There's nothing like the sound of falling snow

The only noise everyone believes
Can make the clock tick slow

A beautiful sound
He sweeps it away
The dimness of city streets

It wraps around my face
With a soft embrace
Almost every state it meets

A sound that's not a falling sound at all
Very quiet, pure
Soft, very well dear

With every fall
It comforts all
Every sleeping soul
Who sit may watch and even here

DREAMING IN THE CLOUDS

I sleep in the clouds up in the sky
I'll keep on dreaming as time passes me by
Each dream keeps me sane
Dreaming of all happiness
A life with no hurt and pain
Family says I'm stuck in this cold place
That I'll never go nowhere

But in my dreams
Like déjà vu
I've been there
I know soon I'll have to wake up
This cruel world feels like a nightmare

So safe with my eyes closed in wonderland
To all the dreamers that know how I feel

No matter what anybody says
Keep on dreaming
But don't dream your life away

BATTERED LOVE

You're the bruises on my collarbones
My stomach, my jaw, and the lower part of my back
Now with every move
I can feel the places your love has left behind

I know you say your body was a broken watch
That your family has worn you down
Now you have become nothing but a ticking time bomb
But know that I love you to the death of me
I wish your eyes could see

Know that I will wait for you
Not for long but in a way a pianist waits for the note
That follows a long night's rest
You are air until you are here with me

Bruised and battered
I will still hold my breath for your love

FINAL DREAMS

Your eyes close
Spread your wings
With one wish, dream good dreams
Never ever say you won't tell

Life is too short, and like elderly, frail
Be very quiet, still, and just look
Take one breath, and you'll be hooked

One blink of an eye
Before you know it, it was all a lie
Look up, and they'll be gone

Hey, two days feel so long
What was once there has disappeared

All along love is the thing to fear

Why say go when it was really no?
When your eyes open, all you'll find
Is what lied there was the only sign
For now, close your eyes and spread your wings
Make one final wish
And forever live all your dreams

NEVER CAN SAY GOODBYE

You never said goodbye
You never said I'm leaving
You never said goodbye
When I looked, you were gone before I knew it

Only Jesus knows why
A million times I needed you
A million times I cried
If my love alone could have saved you
You never would have died

You were my world. I loved you dearly
In death, I love you still
In my heart, a special place you hold
That no one could ever replace
My heart is broken bad to lose you

But you are not there alone
A big part of me left too
The day our God called you home

DEAR LOVED ONES

Hey, I sit in heaven
I'm watching over you every day
The rain is one sign I'm not gone away
You're laughing. I can hear
My eyes are on you when you sleep
I even place my arms around you
To calm you as you weep
Wishing you can go back some days
Begging to have me home
So I send you signs
So you'll know you are not alone
Don't take away your life that was denied to me
Heaven is so beautiful
Wait your turn. You'll see
Go on with life
Laugh some more
Enjoy yourself, live free
For I'll know every breath you take
There's also one taken for me

A MOTHER'S PRAYER

Lord, my children are everything to me
But I doubt my parenting skills
Please guide me every single day to teach them your will

You say train up a child in the way they should go
For as they get older, they'll never part
Lord, they are every piece of my heart

Encouraged by the Lord, always
Live your Christian ways
Walk the path of righteousness
Each and every day

In the almighty name of Jesus, I pray
Amen

I APOLOGIZE

I apologize for everything hurtful I say
I pay for it each and every day
I recognize the mistake after the fact
Never meant it to come out that way
Finally something I can admit

I apologized, but I guess it wasn't enough
Why not let me explain my wrong?
A lot came out from anger, not from love
Please let's start over again

Never knew how to tell you how I feel
Can't imagine my life without you
With you, I'm saying in your love so real
You are the light that shines and keeps me true

I'll understand if you move on without me
I apologize for hurting you in any way
Trust I meant when I said I apologize
Please, baby, I know you won't forget
But forgive me for the things I say

FORGIVING TO FORGET

Laying across my bed, looking at the ceiling
I see a small part of God's plan
Thinking about forgiveness I always had a hard time with
I've been hurt badly in my past
Now scorned
So to be honest
I didn't see fit to let go of the hurt
Karma plays a big part in my life
For the longest time

Sitting for hours
Thinking of different ways to get back at those who hurt me
The thing that brought me to reality
Was Jesus telling me to let go and let God

Forgiveness isn't something that just happens
You must be taught and then practice it

I've got a lot of practice with my family
Sometimes with family, it's a daily task

What we didn't get told was along with forgiving, we have to forget
Why forgive when you're going to bring it up once you forgave them?

It's like you never forgave in the first place
Now I practice both forgiveness and forgetting
It's much simpler now that I let God guide me

I always heard from the Bishop
When I first believed God was in the passenger seat
I learned to move over and let Him drive

He's shown me more than I ever was able to show Him
So if there's trouble with forgiveness
Keep reading verses over and over
Maybe one day they'll make perfect sense to you too

This is how my father treats each of you unless you forgive from your heart

— MATTHEW 18:35 NIV

POOH, MY SON, I OFTEN WISH

I often wish you were still small
Not so big, strong, and tall
Pool when I dream of yesterday
Dark with my eyes close eye vision you playing

I sometimes miss that little boy
Who buttered me up to buy a toy
My heart and days filled with so much light
From the early morning to late hours at night

I watch my Prince change and grow
Every season comes and quickly goes
But Father God has a perfect plan
To shape a gorgeous boy into a handsome man

Today and forever, my son
I'm proud of you for all the thoughtful things you do
I'm going to love you till my life here is done

And even after I'm gone
Be grateful you're my son

NEVER FALL IN LOVE AGAIN

Damn it! I loved you
You hurt me again
Now, this is the third time
I thought I found a lover
Now I'm in bed with another guy
Once again, I have to cry
Telling another lover goodbye

So many nights I cried
I wish I had died
This is my fifth time
Last time I have tried
Why must my relationships always end bad inside?
How many tears must fall from my eyes?
I will never fall in love again

We get a broken heart

How long should I wait for this pain to depart
Love, if you are so nice, why am I sad?
Damn you! I am so mad

I hate you now
I have a score and heart
I don't want love to restart
Look at the tears in my eyes
Even my heart cries

I have been crying so many years
My eyes have run out of tears
This year is too much pain

I will never fall in love
No, not ever again

ALL OF ETERNITY

He has taken me
Now he's claiming me
I've never loved anything or anyone so much
Never wanted for anything to never stop in all my life
As much as I want our love to continue forever
The feeling of fullness
This crazy knowledge
To know this man is all mine
And that I'm all his
So I can give him all of what he wants
What I want to give him is something I never gave anyone
In all the years of my life
Eternity

EVEN THOUGH

My soul is breaking
My mind so unclear
My heart is tired, restless, and full of fear
Stay with me

Even though
I say words I shouldn't
I don't do things I should
You doubt me, and I try to change
But you never think I could
Stay with me

Even though
We thought evil thoughts
We thought over the thoughts again
We turned every thought into an action
Now we have seen

Stay with me

Even though
I said we know each other
We belong together
You don't surprise me by your actions
I created you in my image
I fashioned all with care
I cried tears into my pillow
Remembering you were there
You have always been and say you always will be

When you say those things
I still belong to you
Don't you see?
Even though you still can stay with me

He created a secret place
That you might seek my face
Our Father's warm embrace
Rocking you close to hear your fears

You laid on my lap
So I can wipe your tears
I make all things new to you
Forgiving you, healing you
Just to restore a clean heart in you

Showering your love with grace
Never turn your back to me
So you will see just my face

Our journey home
When you see your run
Even though, my love
Even though
Just stay

YOU ME

I don't wanna fancy dinner
Or a Hollywood date
I just want to eat overcooked noodles
Sitting on your counter
Laughing at the faces we make

Stripping down to underwear
And watching Kung Fu movies with you naked beside me
Let's have popcorn in sugar
Not ever worrying about saying goodbyes

Not asking for much
Just all your love with no lies

MY PRECIOUS CHILD

My precious child
Our beautiful baby
Dearly held to my heart
You'll always be with me

A duty and an important job
Or journey just for you
So much love to give and work to do

A borrowed angel
Beautiful, smart, and small to shine
Bright on family and gives so much
Love all before he takes you home

I want you to hold this

A piece of my heart
Not several but one last kiss
We know you still close
That I know
The book told me so
But our Lord shows you
With one wing to heaven
You must go

CRYING ON THE INSIDE

You'll never see this hell
I'm lost because all I do is laugh

So many ways
I don't want you to notice
My life is so torn
You're too good for my problems

Why am I still screaming for you to rescue me?
I'm crying on the inside for help
Right in front of your face
But you can't help because I'm on the out

I have to laugh to keep from crying

AFRAID OF BEING ME

All these guys you see
Every one of them made by me

My eyes are bloody red
From the mini tears, I have shared
I feel lost in this madness
But I'm all choked up with sadness
I've tried pills, also tried a knife
Looking back now on my whole life
So much pain, so much dying hurt

My heart felt like it was going to burst
I yelled, screen, and had a furious outburst

Now the can is flowing
Why couldn't they just see
That my entire life
I was really afraid of being me?

MASTERPIECE EYES

My tears run down my face
They drip off my nose
In dark corners I cry where really nobody goes
Follow the marks from my eyes down my chin
Month after month of letting it win
In my eyes, there's a story with nothing but anger in pain
The smile makes it seem like I'm happy
Stop and look again
My scars from my past are hidden underneath my clothes
It's like MapQuest to places that nobody knows
This smile is now permanently painted
I'm now a master of a good disguise
You see it all
Just stop and take a look into my brown eyes

SHE RAN

She ran along this quiet street
No one to wipe her tears
Wishing someone was there to rub her feet
Maybe just to take away her fears

Dealing with life with a scorned heart
Every day is gloomy and grey
Always alone, a new start seems far apart
Constantly in search of a way

Life must go on no matter what
The fact she always balls
No memories to be forgotten
Deep in her heart, they dwell

She kept running this quiet street
Kept coming up short with no way
Every so often, she dressed with no sleep
Always praying he soon brings a better day

MAMA, THANKS

She walked beside me
My momma held my precious hand
She taught me so many things that I didn't understand

Taught me to be safe from strangers every day
Told me don't give up but give it my best
Whether home or school at play

Every child needs a gentle hand to guide them as they grow
Thanks for walking by me
My momma
Now I'm a momma and have such a long journey to go

ENOUGH PAIN!

I sat alone
Alone in my home
Where my screams for help were silent
My mind thought of nothing but violence

My insecurities were never deep inside
So they didn't eat me alive
As tears roll down my face faster
My skin began to raise
So I took a blade and slit my skin

Where my depression lies deep within
It lasted so many days, months, even years
Finally, I cried my last tears

Yes, world, for me, it was enough
Everything around me was too tough
I placed the loaded gun to my head
Thanks to this society
No more pain
I'm dead

LOVE PAIN

The thing about pain from love
It never lasts forever
And it may kill you right now
Indeed time gets better
The thing about love scars
They all eventually will fade
Until nothing is left of the marks that may have been made
This thing about life today
It will always be a better tomorrow
So if you can't find a smile
Mine you can always borrow
The thing about help is
Beside you, it will stand
It doesn't know its use is needed
You must reach out your hand
The thing about God's love is
You can't feel His touch
You must let Him know
That this painful world is too much

NO GOODBYES

You may soon find me one morning
My heart will no longer be
Please don't say it's tragic
Don't lie saying I had so much to live for

Ask why I left so soon
Just burn me up
Start a good fire
Matter of fact, bury me in the backyard

Kissing me goodbye through the wind
That can be the end
All my memories become a distant fire dream

Not a nightmare, a dream of only a dream

Knocked down my door like it was empty there
Make it vanish
Cut me out of all the pictures

Burn my letters with me in them
Just don't say it was a tragedy
That the thumping in my chest stopped beating

Instead, forget about me
Don't make my spirit haunt you

I'M TIRED

I'm tired of running from it
Always falling a step behind
The worst part is now I'm trapped in my own mind
I'm tired now
The end is near
Really I can't keep trying
Please stop asking me if I'm OK
Truly I'm just tired of lying

This fake smile is getting so heavy
I'm tired of these tears
My eyes can't hold back
Now my tired mind has finally won
Done living in a world that's black

Jesus, I'm tired of going through these motions

Now, in the end, it's time to quit
People mostly fear death
When tired like me
I pray for it

MY OUTBURST OF CRY

It's a big deal of depression
Taking over my soul
Deep down within every ounce
That makes me whole

Often wonder and worry throughout the day
I'll wait on it to come to my dismay

Tears flood my eyes with all expressions
More than normal with more depressions

Convincing myself everything is gonna be ok
But really, for real, who am I fooling?
I have so much anger; I'm enraged
So many questions, but really there is no answer

I'm afraid and so weak
Why try to explain?
All I hear is I'm wrong in need to seek
No, this is how I'm feeling
Remember there is no wrong or right

Wait while I battle with fears myself
No matter if I lose the fight
Never intimidated by others

Like I said, this is just how I feel
All this pain in me is so real
Lose all control
My thoughts gone wild
And I'm not an only child

If only you knew my thoughts
Only if you knew battles are fought
In need of my thoughts held captive

Dear Lord, assure me my thoughts are normal
You got them on a positive track
I'm crying for help
I need you
Never give me up soon
One day I will forever make you smile

Thanks,
Not Only Your Child

NOT WORTH IT

Say it to be the type of person that always held onto things
To fight
Never want to release my grip if it no longer felt right
Although it gave me blisters
My fingers would always ache

I always thought that holding on
Really was worth the pain it takes
I used to think I was losing things
I was losing part of me too

Soon, slowly, I'll be someone
My heart no longer knew
One day something bad happened
Lost what I once held dear
But my heart became much lighter
Instead of filled with fear

It taught my heart that some things were never meant to last long
They visit to teach us lessons
Then they move on
Never have to cling to people
That no longer make you smile
Always doing some things you now hate
Even if it's not worth your while

Sometimes the things you fight for
Are really not worth the cost
So not everything you lose is bound to be a loss

THOUGHTS OF YOU

I'm thinking of you today
But that's nothing new
I thought of you yesterday
And the days before that too
Each and every day
Good or bad, forever in my head

Please understand every word I've said
Not a joke or a simple lie
Would never do anything to make you cry
Apologize when I do something to make you really mad

It only reverts back to make me really sad
I do love you and everything you are
Hoping this relationship gets us far
My system
Never can get you out

Simply do not know how

I'm thinking of you right now
Definitely everything I need
Really everything to me
You know exactly who you are
And what you mean to me

Always was making me smile just by being there
Don't you know how much I really care?
Every time you're on my mind

This is why I love you
I made this list
It goes on forever and will never end
Neither will this love
You'll always be my homie lover friend
Not just any friend, but that special friend
And for that reason
I've wanted to always spend my whole life
Only with you

ONCE WAS BLIND OF YOUR LOVE

I was lonely for so long
No one there I could love
Waiting for a special someone
To come down from heaven above

Special someone to share my heart with
Hold me all through the night
That's here for me to tell my problems and worries to
Finally love with all my might

No doubt ever about how I wanted
True love to finally come my way
I must have been awaiting your love
So from now on I can truly say

You were the one I always wanted forever
You forever will mean the world to me
I always have been awaiting your love
Once was blind, but now I see